My World

MY FAMILY

By Gladys Rosa-Mendoza • Illustrations by Jackie Snider

WINDMILL
BOOKS
New York

Published in 2011 by Windmill Books, LLC
303 Park Avenue South, Suite # 1280, New York, NY 10010-3657

Adaptations to North American Edition © 2011 Windmill Books, LLC
First published by me+mi publishing, inc. © 2001
Text and illustrations copyright © me+mi publishing, inc., 2001

CREDITS:
Author: Gladys Rosa-Mendoza
Illustrator: Jackie Snider

Library of Congress Cataloging-in-Publication Data

Rosa-Mendoza, Gladys.
  My family / by Gladys Rosa-Mendoza ; illustrated by Jackie Snider. — School and library ed.
     p. cm. — (My world)
  Earlier ed. published as: My family and I = Mi familia y yo.
  Includes index.
  ISBN 978-1-60754-946-8 (library binding) — ISBN 978-1-61533-025-6 (pbk.) — ISBN 978-1-61533-026-3 (6-pack)
  1. Families—Juvenile literature. I. Snider, Jackie. II. Rosa-Mendoza, Gladys. My family and I. III. Title.
  HQ744.R67 2010
  306.85—dc22
                              2009054401

Manufactured in the United States of America

For more great fiction and nonfiction, go to www.windmillbooks.com.

CPSIA Compliance Information: Batch #S10W: For further information contact Windmill Books, New York, New York at 1-866-478-0556.

Contents

Hello, my name is Emma. Come with me and meet my family.

This is my mom.

This is my dad.

They are making lunch together.

This is my brother.

This is my sister.

This is my dog.

This is my cat.

I love to play with them.

This is my grandmother.

This is my grandfather.

I love to visit
with them.

These are my aunts.
They are putting
flowers in a vase.

These are my uncles. They are making music.

These are
my cousins.

We are playing
in the backyard.

Here we are having dinner together.

18

This is my family!

Read More!

Nonfiction

Adamson, Heather. *Families in Many Cultures*. Mankato, MN: Pebble Plus, 2009.

Moore-Mallinos, Jennifer. *My Grandparents Are Special*. Hauppauge, NY: Barron's Educational Series, 2006.

Fiction

Numeroff, Laura. *Would I Trade My Parents?* New York: Abrams Books for Young Readers, 2009.

Simon, Norma. *All Families Are Special*. Park Ridge, IL: Albert Whitman & Company, 2003.

Wilson, Adrienne C. *Isaac and the Bah Family Tree*. Mustang, OK: Tate Publishing, 2008.

Learn More!

 All families are different. Sometimes a family lives together. Sometimes family members live far away from each other.

 We call our parents' moms and dads our grandparents.

 One woman had 69 children. That is a world record!

Who is in your family?
What makes your family special?

Words to Know

aunt (ant) your mother or father's sister

cousin (KUH-zin) the children of your aunts and uncles

brother (BRUH-thur) a boy who has the same parents as you

dog (dahg) a four-legged furry animal related to the wolf

cat (kat) a small four-legged furry animal related to the lion and tiger

family (FA-mih-lee) a group of people related by blood or marriage

father (FAH-thur) a man who has children

mother (MUH-thur) a woman who has children

grandfather (GRAND-fah-thur) your mother or father's father

sister (SIS-tur) a girl who has the same parents as you

grandmother (GRAND-muh-thur) your mother or father's mother

uncle (UNG-kul) your mother or father's brother

Index

Web Sites

For Web resources related to the subject of this book, go to:
www.windmillbooks.com/weblinks and select this book's title.